Hamster

Written by
Matthew Rayner BVetMed MRCVS

Photographed by
Frank Greenaway

Gareth Stevens Publishing
A WORLD ALMANAC EDUCATION GROUP COMPANY

Please visit our web site at: www.garethstevens.com
For a free color catalog describing Gareth Stevens
Publishing's list of high-quality books and multi-
media programs, call 1-800-542-2595 (USA)
or 1-800-387-3178 (Canada). Gareth Stevens
Publishing's fax: (414) 332-3567.

Library of Congress Cataloging-in-Publication Data

Rayner, Matthew.
      Hamster / written by Matthew Rayner;
  photographed by Frank Greenaway. — North
  American ed.
          p. cm. — (I am your pet)
      Includes bibliographical references and index.
      Summary: Presents simple information about
  hamsters and choosing one as a pet.
      ISBN 0-8368-4104-2 (lib. bdg.)
      1. Hamsters as pets—Juvenile literature.
  [1. Hamsters. 2. Pets.] I. Greenaway, Frank, ill.
  II. Title.
  SF459.H3R38   2004
  636.935'6—dc22   2003066153

This North American edition first published in 2004 by
Gareth Stevens Publishing
A World Almanac Education Group Company
330 West Olive Street, Suite 100
Milwaukee, WI 53212 USA

Original edition copyright © 2004 Bookwork Ltd.,
Unit 17, Piccadilly Mill, Lower Street,
Stroud, Gloucestershire, GL5 2HT,
United Kingdom.

Editorial Director: Louise Pritchard
Editor: Annabel Blackledge
Design Director: Jill Plank
Art Editor: Kate Mullins
Gareth Stevens Editor:
  Jenette Donovan Guntly
Gareth Stevens Designer:
  Kami M. Koenig

Printed in the United States of America

1 2 3 4 5 6 7 8 9 08 07 06 05 04

Picture credits
t=top, b=bottom, m=middle, l=left, r=right
All photographs by Frank Greenaway except for the
following: P & S Charmley: 7tr, 7ml, 7mt, 7mb, 7br, 26t,
29t, 29m; Warren Photographic: 8–9b, 27r, 28l, 28–29m

Ooooh,
is this book all
about me?

Contents

Words that appear in the glossary are printed in **boldface** type the first time they are used in the text.

My family

I come from a family of animals called **rodents**. Mice and rats are some of my closest cousins. People call me a Syrian or Golden hamster. There are lots of other **breeds** of pet hamster, but I am the most popular.

Racing heart

My tiny heart beats between three hundred and five hundred times a minute — that is about five times faster than yours!

Tiny tail

My tail is so tiny, you can hardly see it!

Toes

I have five toes on each back paw.

This is me

Hip spots

I have a small spot on each hip. I use these spots to mark my home with a special scent.

Life story

I was fully grown when I was about three months old. I am about 7 inches (17 centimeters) long and I weigh about 4 ounces (125 grams). I will probably live until I am two or three years old. That is a lot of time for fun!

Hamster sense
My eyesight is bad, but I can hear and smell better than you can.

I just can't help being so cute!

Teeth
I may look cute, but my mouth is full of strong, sharp teeth!

Fingers
I have four fingers on each front paw.

Fat face
Do not worry if my face looks fat and lumpy. I have **pouches** in my cheeks that I use to hold food and **bedding**.

All shapes

Furry friends

My hamster friends come in all shapes and sizes. There are tiny dwarf hamsters, Russian hamsters, Chinese hamsters, hairy hamsters, spotted hamsters — and even hamsters that change color!

I think I am in pretty good shape!

Golden hamster

You will probably see lots of hamsters like me in pet shops. Most Syrians have beautiful golden coats like mine. I make a good pet because I do not bite often and I like to be picked up.

Dwarf hamsters

Dwarf hamsters are my smallest friends and they come in all sorts of colors. All dwarf hamsters are related to Dwarf Russian hamsters.

and sizes

Campbell's Dwarf
This little hamster has hairy feet.

Winter Whites
These dwarf hamsters' coats sometimes turn pure white in the winter.

Perfect pets
All hamsters like to eat, sleep, and play. We all make good pets, too. Dwarfs can be hard to catch, so Syrians suit new owners best.

Dove
This Syrian is a rare dove color. She stands out from the crowd!

Chocolate tort
This Syrian is called a **chocolate tort**. He is brown with a white band around his belly.

A coat for all occasions

Long coats, short coats, smooth coats, fluffy coats — we hamsters have it all. Some coats are rare, but if you search hard, you will find the perfect hamster.

Teddy bear
This fluffy Syrian is known as a "teddy bear" hamster.

Wild life

Eating and sleeping

My wild hamster relatives live in the desert and spend most of their time searching for food. They look for food at night, when it is not too hot. They sleep during the day.

Taste of freedom
Like my wild cousins, I love searching and sniffing for food. If you hide things like nuts and seeds around my cage, I will hunt happily for hours.

Large litters
Wild female hamsters usually have eight babies. But they can have as many as twenty-five!

Staying together
Wild Syrian hamsters stay with their family until they are five or six weeks old. Then, they go off on their own.

Finding food
Wild hamsters use their good sense of smell to find food.

Wild at heart

Like wild hamsters, I am sleepy in the daytime and awake at night. I am happiest when I am busy. I am good at caring for myself, too.

Keeping clean
I lick my paws and rub them on my fur to keep it clean.

Mmmm, I can smell breakfast.

The basics

Before you buy me and take me home, you must get everything I need. A cage, bedding, some food, and a water bottle are most important. You can always get the extras later.

Safe house

If you have a cat, a cage with solid sides is best. Cages like this also suit my dwarf friends, who can slip between the bars of other cages.

Escape artist

I am extremely good at escaping. I can squeeze through tiny spaces and even pile up my bedding so that I can reach the top of my cage.

Be prepared

House hunting

Hamster cages come in all shapes and sizes. Buy me a home that is easy to clean, secure, roomy, and airy. Then, I will be safe and comfortable.

Tunnels and tubes

I love crawling through tunnels. It is like being a wild hamster tunneling through the sand.

Ahhh, that was a wonderful nap!

Which bedding?
I like my cage to be lined with a thick layer of aspen wood shavings. I also need a cosy pile of soft, shredded tissues or clean **hay** inside my house.

Shredded paper

Hay

Aspen wood shavings

Hamster house
I need somewhere dark and warm in my cage where I can sleep and store my food. A house like this is perfect.

Bedtime
If I wake up during the day, I can get grumpy. Put my cage in a quiet place and give me a house to hide in.

Food and water
I need food and fresh water at all times. A water bottle fixed to my cage is best, so I cannot spill it.

A little air
I do not like wind or drafts, but I do need fresh air. A cage with both solid sides and some narrow bars will suit me best.

The right

I see you!
Look for a hamster that is playful and active. If he is curious about you when you look into his cage, he will most likely be affectionate and friendly to you at home.

Mmmm, I could lie here all day.

Finding your hamster
You can buy a hamster from a **breeder**. You can also find hamsters for sale in notices at pet shops and in newspapers. If you cannot find any, buy your hamster from a pet shop with a very good reputation.

The right time
The best time to choose a hamster is late afternoon. Hamsters will be sleepy earlier in the day and might not feel like saying hello to you.

choice

LOOK OUT!
- **Be very** careful when you buy your hamster. If his cage is dirty or the hamsters look sick or are very young, do not buy one. Try somewhere else.

Please take me home with you . . .

Pick me!
I have bright, clear eyes. I also have a clean bottom, mouth, and nose. I am nice and plump. Make sure the hamster you choose looks as healthy as I do.

Nice natured
Hamsters like me make perfect pets. I am friendly and not too shy.

Eating habits

Like a wild hamster, I am happy to try all sorts of different foods. You do not have to feed me at the same time every day, but please make sure there is always some food in my cage. My favorite time to eat is at night, when you are fast asleep in bed.

Feeding time!

Peanuts

Pellets

Flaked corn

Locust bean chips

Secret snacks

I like to collect food in my cheek pouches. When they are full, I empty them in a quiet corner. Then, I can have a little nibble when no one is watching.

Flaked peas

A little variety
I like to eat a good mixture of different seeds and **grains**. The variety helps me to stay interested in my food.

Wheat

Sunflower seeds

In the mix

You can buy hamster mix in pet shops. It should include things like wheat, corn, sunflower seeds, peanuts, and special hamster food pellets.

Yum, I think I'll save this for later.

Tasty treats
Hamsters can eat some human foods such as breakfast cereal, natural yogurt, and toast. Give us only a tiny bit at a time, though.

LOOK OUT!
- **Do not feed** me onions, **citrus fruits**, raw potato, or plants such as buttercups, because they will make me sick.
- **Never feed** me chocolate, potato chips, or sweet foods. No matter how nice they taste, they could make me sick.

Fruits and veggies
We love things like bananas, apples, cucumbers, raw peas, carrots, and green beans. We also like to eat a little fresh hay and grass. You can give us a small piece of fresh food every day.

Water, water!
I do not usually drink much water each day, but you should still fill my bottle with fresh water. Keep an eye on how much I am drinking. If I suddenly start to drink a lot, it could be a sign that I am not very well.

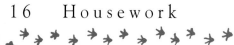

Housework

Safe place
Be sure to put me in a safe place while you clean my cage.

> I am coming back. Are you ready?

Clean routine
You must keep my cage nice and clean so that it does not start to smell or become full of **germs**. Take out any uneaten fresh food every day because it will go bad.

Washing up

Wash my cage and house properly at least once a week. Use a mild dish soap to wash them. Never use bleach. Rinse and dry my cage thoroughly.

Making my bed

When you change my nesting material, please leave it outside my house. I like to make my own bed. I drag the bedding into my house and tunnel through it to fluff it up.

Out with the old

Throw away the wood shavings from the floor of my cage. Save a little of the nesting material so that the cage still smells like me.

In with the new

Wash and dry my cage and house. Then, replace the wood shavings. Last of all, give me a small pile of new nesting material.

LOOK OUT!

- **Do not** leave me with wet bedding. Replace it as soon as you notice it.
- **On cleaning** day, throw away the old food in my cage. Moldy food might make me sick.

Back where I belong

When you put me back in my cage, leave me alone for a few hours. I like time to settle in again.

Many moods

Like you, I have different moods and my own funny little ways. Sometimes I feel grumpy or shy, and sometimes I feel like being naughty. You can often guess my mood from the way I behave and move.

Body talk

Curious creature

When I am curious, I open my eyes wide and move around a lot. I sniff things in my path and investigate everywhere. I act like this only when I am happy and relaxed.

Taste test
If I am feeling really curious, I might investigate things with my teeth.

Fight or flight?
If I am angry or scared, I will usually try to run away. If I cannot escape, I may curl up in a ball or roll away from the scary thing. If I am feeling really brave, I may try to fight or bite.

Tired and grumpy
I can get very grumpy when I am woken up at the wrong time. If my ears are flat and my eyes are half closed, this is a sign to leave me alone.

Under investigation
I might decide to investigate you. My feet and nose will tickle a bit!

LOOK OUT!
• **Do not** pick me up after you have eaten. My sense of smell is good but my eyesight is not, and I may mistake your finger for some food. I am not being naughty. I am just confused.

Busy body
When I feel like it, I can move very fast! I can squeeze into places much smaller than you would think.

Scent spreading
When I am out of my cage, I may go to the bathroom a lot. I do not mean to be messy. I am just spreading my scent around.

Mischievous . . . who, me?

Feeling silly
I can be **mischievous** when I am in the mood. I might kick my bedding out of my cage. Or, I might show off by getting into funny places and positions.

Hold me close

Once I am used to you feeding and stroking me, you can try to pick me up. Scoop me up gently and cup me in both hands. Do not squeeze me too hard or lift me up high.

Don't hug me too hard. I am only little!

Wriggly worm
I can be very wriggly, so be careful not to drop me.

Try again later
If I am very wriggly, it may mean I am scared. Put me back in my cage and try again later.

Making friends

Hand feeding

You can gain my trust by letting me eat food from your hands. To help me get used to your smell and touch, rest your hand inside my cage. I will soon investigate.

Tempting treats
When I am really tame, you can feed me while you are holding me.

I wonder what games we'll play tomorrow.

Toothy tip
I bite only if I am scared. All I need is a little bit of time to get used to you. If you are worried about my teeth, try wearing gloves to handle me at first.

Faithful friend

Soon, I will learn when to expect you to come to see me. I might even be waiting for you when you come to feed or play with me. You are my best friend after all!

Fun and

Going nowhere fast

Even if you play with me every evening, I will still spend a lot of time in my cage. Give me an exercise wheel so that I can go for a run whenever I feel like it. Then I will not get too fat.

Safety first
My wheel must be solid so my legs do not get caught.

Disappearing act
If you let me out of my cage, you will need to watch me closely. Keep me shut in one safe room. If you do not, you may have to play a long game of hide-and-seek. I love to squeeze into tiny places out of your reach!

games

Busy is best

Wild hamsters can travel up to 5 miles (8 kilometers) looking for food. If I am left in my cage with nothing to do, I might get bored. I will probably do my best to escape.

You know, I think I might . . .

LOOK OUT!
- **When you** put me away, make sure my cage is closed, or I might escape!
- **When I** am out of my cage, keep other pets away from me. Do not let me get inside vents, closets, or drawers. Be sure I do not eat things I should not or chew on wires.

Next stop, the kitchen!

. . . have come this way before!

Up, up, and away
I am very good at climbing. I love cages with more than one level. I can even climb up vertical tubes and up curtains in your home. The only problem is that I am not so good at getting down again afterward!

Room to roam
I love cages that are made up of rooms joined by tunnels. By the time I have explored everywhere, I have forgotten where I started from!

Healthy

Health matters

Check me over every evening. If you are worried about me, take me to see a **veterinarian**, or vet, especially if my tummy is upset or I stop eating or drinking. The vet will tell you how to care for me until I am well again.

Paws and claws

Check my feet every evening. If I get lots of exercise, my claws should not get too long. As I grow older and less active, I may need to visit a vet to get my claws clipped.

Acting funny

If I seem quieter or grumpier than usual, it might mean I am sick or injured. Keep a close eye on me. If I do not get well quickly, take me to a vet.

Hamsters

The brush-off
Groom me gently with an old toothbrush. This is a good time to check that my skin and fur are healthy. It feels nice, too!

Something to nibble
A hamster's teeth never stop growing. We need to chew things to stop our teeth from getting too long. Fruit-tree twigs make ideal chewing sticks.

Oooh, stop! That really tickles!

Tip-top shape
Watch me every day to make sure I am my usual self. Check that I am not scratching and have not lost any of my fur. I should have a clean bottom and clear, bright eyes.

Ear, ear
Gently fold back my ear flaps and look in my ears. Make sure they are clean and not sore.

Good company

Group hug
My Dwarf Russian friends like to cuddle up.

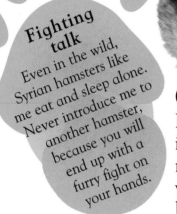

Fighting talk
Even in the wild, Syrian hamsters like me eat and sleep alone. Never introduce me to another hamster, because you will end up with a furry fight on your hands.

Close companions
Dwarf hamsters can live together if they meet at a young age. Do not mix boys and girls because you will have a whole family of hamsters to care for!

Solitary Syrian
I do not like living with other hamsters, so I need you to be my best friend. I will depend on you for everything.

LOOK OUT!

- **Never leave** me alone for more than twenty-four hours. I will need fresh water and food, exercise, and someone to play with. If you go on vacation, you will need to arrange for someone to look after me.

Friends for life
A puppy will get used to me more quickly than an older dog will.

You're a funny looking puppy!

Not my friends
I do not get along well with rats, gerbils, or mice. We may fight. Cats are not friends of mine either. They might decide to eat me!

Little and large
I will probably get along best with a dog, but never leave us alone together. Even a friendly dog could hurt me by mistake because I am so small.

Do you want to share my treat?

Having babies

New arrivals

When hamsters are four to six months old, they can have babies, or pups. The female is pregnant for about sixteen days. Then, she gives birth to the pups — usually between eight and ten of them. The female cares for the babies and feeds them with her milk.

Early days
This is one of my friends at three days old. She was blind, deaf, and hairless, and needed to stay close to her mom.

On the move
After twelve days, she could hear and had grown soft fur. She was still blind, but had begun to move around more.

Bigger and braver
At sixteen days, my friend had a full coat and could see. She was big enough to explore.

Mom's the word
When a hamster is pregnant, she builds a nest. Leave her nest and bedding alone during this time. If you touch the nest, her bedding, or her pups, she may reject them.

Leaving mom
At three weeks, she left her mom and lived with her sisters. Her brothers lived in a separate cage.

My own space
Hamsters are ready to leave their family when they are six weeks old. I did not miss my family when I left it, because I like to have my own space.

LOOK OUT!
• **Do not let** your hamster have babies unless you are sure you can find good homes for them. There are already plenty of hamsters looking for homes. You will need to learn a lot about hamsters before you are ready to help your hamster care for her babies.

Glossary

bedding
Bedding is the material used to line a hamster's cage and house.

breeder
A breeder raises hamsters. A good hamster breeder does not breed a lot of animals and does not sell the animals to pet shops.

breeds
Breeds are types of hamsters. Syrians and Dwarf Russians are just two breeds of hamsters.

chocolate tort
In everyday life, a chocolate torte is a dessert. In hamsters, it means he has chocolate tortoiseshell (tort) fur, meaning a combination of brown and white fur.

citrus fruits
Citrus fruits include grapefruits, oranges, limes, and lemons. They can make hamsters very sick.

germs
Germs are living things. When you do not clean your hamster's cage, germs grow and they can make your hamster sick.

grains
You can buy a special mix of grains, including oats, alfalfa, and wheat, at a pet store. Do not feed your hamster raw grains.

groom
To groom is to gently brush an animal's fur to remove dirt.

hay
Hay is dried grass. Timothy and alfalfa hay are good choices.

mischievous
When a hamster is mischievous, he is feeling playful and naughty.

pouches
Pouches are special pockets in a hamster's cheeks that she uses to hold food and bedding.

rodents
Hamsters belong to the family of animals called rodents. Mice, rats, and gerbils are also rodents.

veterinarian (vet)
A veterinarian, or vet, is a doctor for animals. Take your hamster to see a vet if she is sick or injured.

Find out more . . .

Web Sites

www.animaland.org
This web site for the American
Society for the Prevention of
Cruelty to Animals (ASPCA)
has games, cartoons, a pet care
guide, and much more!

Books

Hamsters. Susan Meredith
(Educational Development
Corporation)

*Hamtaro Hamster Care
Guide.* Ritsuko Kawai
(Viz Communications)

Wow!
I'm famous!

**users.ilnk.com/health/
henrietta**
This web site tells you all about
Henrietta the Hamster. It also
has lots of great photographs
and good information.

www.hamsterhideout.com
This web site is full of useful
information about hamsters,
as well as games, pictures,
resources, and a fun quiz.

Index